I0528623

Harmony

CULTIVATING INNER PEACE

JACKIE GOUCHÉ

KP PUBLISHING COMPANY

ISBN: 978-1-960001-48-1 (Paperback)
ISBN: 978-1-960001-49-8 (Ebook)
Library of Congress Control Number: Pending

Editor: Frank Williams
Cover Design: Osakwe Eseohe Gift
Literary Director: Sandra Slayton James

Published by:

KP Publishing Company
Publisher of Fiction, Nonfiction & Children's Books
Valencia, CA 91355
www.kp-pub.com

Printed in the United States of America

CONTENTS

DEDICATION vii

PREFACE ix

CHAPTER ONE: The Program 1

CHAPTER TWO: I AM 13

CHAPTER THREE: Love vs. Fear 23

CHAPTER FOUR: Acceptance 35

CHAPTER FIVE: Perspective 47

CHAPTER SIX: The Physiology of Harmony 57

CHAPTER SIX: The Power of Music 63

CONCLUSION 71

ABOUT THE AUTHOR 75

DEDICATION

Everyone who knows me is aware that I adore my sons, my KINGS! Since they came into my life, they have been the motivation behind everything I've accomplished. My babies were the reason I conquered addiction. They were the inspiration behind my will to make something great of my life. I wanted them to be proud of me. I still want them to be proud of me.

Ron Ron, when we met in 1983, you took ownership of a piece of my heart, and you hold it firmly to this day. It's an honor for you to call me your mother.

Davion, my firstborn, I didn't really understand *love* until you arrived. Your little chocolate face, black, curly hair and plump, purple lips captured my heart the moment I laid eyes on you. I was in awe of the beauty that Ronald and I had produced. At the age of five, I recognized your amazing gift. I was mesmerized by your voice, and I am still mesmerized to this day.

Daniel aka, D Smoke, my middle son. Astounded by your strength, determination, and wisdom. You have been a *friend* to me since you were old enough to talk. A leader, teacher, and mentor to many, I cannot tell you how proud I am of the great man that you have become. Your commitment to excellence is evident and inspiring. What a joy to be your mother!

Sir Darryl, my youngest son. Your unique style of being is a beautiful thing to behold. You always have been your own man. An independent thinker. I get the greatest joy watching you navigate your life, your way. You've overcome extraordinary challenges, and transformed yourself into the wonderful son, father, brother, and friend that you are. My pride in being your mother is unmatched!

My sons, *my* kings, this book is dedicated to you!

PREFACE

*"There are three constants in life; change,
choice, and principles."*
—Stephen Covey

Harmony can be defined as a consistent, orderly, or pleasing arrangement of parts. When the word **harmony** is used, most people think of music. In my case, that was true for most of my life. I learned the theory behind musical harmony at an early age. In 1975, my mother taught my brothers and I to sing three-part harmony on a song called 'Say You Love Me' by DJ Rogers. My soul bubbled with excitement at the blending of three voices into one sound. I fell in love with that feeling and ultimately became a master at creating and executing intricate harmonies. I was able to make a decent living with that skill set. But while I was mastering the art of musical harmony, and even working on having harmonious relationships with those around me, I had no idea of the importance of harmony within myself. Inner harmony is a state of peace that arises when our thoughts, emotions, desires, and actions are in alignment. I wish I could say that this is something I learned and practiced early in life, but the truth is, I was in my late fifties when I came to this understanding.

Have you ever been at odds with yourself? Do you sometimes find yourself doing things you'd rather not be doing, or engaging in activities in which you see no real value, but you do them anyway out of social pressure? Like going out for a drink with friends when you really don't like the taste of alcohol. Are you often disappointed in yourself or frustrated with your own choices and behavior? Well, my friend, you are not alone.

Until recently, I lived in opposition to myself. I would often say "yes" when there was a resounding "no" ringing in my soul. I would make choices based on what others expected of me rather than what I truly desired. Even my desires were based on what others told me I needed. I was always trying to prove my worth by being the best at what

I did, and carefully cultivating relationships with others, but my relationship with myself was floundering. My thoughts, desires and actions were rarely in sync, and as a result, inner peace or *harmony* was always just beyond my reach.

Throughout my entire life, my priorities were always based on someone else's opinion. However, after a lifetime of low self-esteem, people-pleasing, self-sacrificing, non-confrontational acquiescence, I finally found the courage to begin my journey of self-discovery, self-care, and self-love.

As you read these words, you will come closer to understanding how you became the person that you are. Then you will learn steps to aid you in becoming the person that you truly desire to be. In the pages to follow, I will share with you the lessons and principles that I learned in over fifty years of pain and suffering, trial and error, tragedy, and triumph.

Before I begin, I'd first like to take a moment and emphasize the power of "spiritual laws." They are fixed, immutable truths that provide the framework upon which the universe operates. Everyone is familiar with natural laws such as the law of gravity. Before we get behind the wheel of a car, we are taught the laws that govern the road. But too many people are attempting to navigate life without being aware of the laws that govern it. It's like trying to drive without knowing the difference between a red light and a green one. You might make it a block or two but, eventually, you are bound to crash.

In the early nineties, when I was a single mom to my four-, five- and six-year-old sons, disorganization, frustration, and overwhelm was the theme of my life. I would overbook myself and miss appointments, bounce checks, and pay overdraft fees. I knew I needed help, but I didn't know where to begin. Believing that I could find answers in books, I went to that section of the local Target, and was led to pick up a book called *The Ten Natural Laws of Successful Time and Life Management* by Hyrum Smith. This was the beginning of my self-improvement/self-help journey. I devoured the contents of this book and immediately began implementing its principles. In approximately eighteen months, I was able to set and achieve goals, create a budget, raise my credit score, purchase my first, brand new vehicle without a co-signer, all while working as a background vocalist, minister of music, and a single parent. I was even able to spend quality time with my little guys. It was my understanding of, and adherence to spiritual laws that enabled me to take full responsibility for my circumstances and navigate a successful path.

Read this book carefully. Ingest, and digest its contents. When applied, these principles will only serve to enhance the quality of your life. My sincere hope is that you don't have to wait until your "golden years" to experience true harmony.

Chapter One

THE PROGRAM

*"Give me a child until he is seven years old,
and I will show you the man."*
—ARISTOTLE

Jennifer and Brianna have a lot in common. They are both seventeen, live in the same neighborhood and attend the same high school. Each of them lives in the home with both parents and a younger sibling, but that is where their similarities end. Jennifer is a gifted, bubbly, compassionate young lady who exudes confidence. Her father is a warm, loving and patient man who adores his children and takes personal responsibility for their happiness. He often takes them hiking, fishing and horseback riding. Jennifer also plays the violin, and her dad is her biggest fan. He refers to

1

her as his "little princess" and never misses a recital. Jennifer's mother is a stay-at-home mom, who's number one priority is the health and well-being of her children. She loves to cook and teaches them the importance of eating healthy.

Brianna's story is a bit different from Jennifer's. Brianna's father is a functional alcoholic who has a standing appointment at the local bar when he leaves work. Most days, he waits until his wife is asleep before coming home to avoid the inevitable castigation he's sure to receive. Brianna's mother works for the post office and is very unhappy in her marriage. She spends most of her days complaining to anyone who will listen about her husband and his drinking habit. She faults him for the failure of their marriage and takes no responsibility for her own actions. Whenever Brianna's parents are in the same room, a fight is sure to ensue. As far back as she can remember, Brianna has spent much of her time in her bedroom, with headphones and a pillow over her head. It was never enough to completely drown out the sound of her parents yelling at one another.

For the first seven years of her life, Jennifer's parents were often doting over her and telling her how special she was. Accustomed to hearing words like, *pretty*, *smart*, *precious*, *brilliant*, and *gifted*, Jennifer developed a healthy sense of self-esteem and self-worth. Her parents placed the violin in her little hands at the age of three. And even when the screeching sound of her practicing was almost unbearable, they encouraged her and told her what a great job she was doing. Now, in high school, Jennifer is a master-violinist. She is also a cheerleader and a member of the debate team. Jennifer has already been accepted to several colleges, including UCLA, and has only to decide which one she wants to attend. She plans on majoring in Political Science.

Brianna's story is quite the opposite. She was placed in day-care when she was only two months old so her mother could return to work. For the next seven years, her life consisted mainly of school, babysitters, and McDonald's happy meals. At home, she was accustomed to hearing things like *"shut-up and sit down," "because I said so," "go to your room,"* and *"don't ask stupid questions."* With a constant diet of negativity, and a complete lack of nurturing, Brianna suffers with low self-esteem and seeks refuge in drugs and alcohol. She lost her virginity at the age of 13 and has become quite promiscuous due to her parents' neglect.

Every word that Jennifer heard from the day she was born to the age of 7 became a part of her "truth," her belief system, her narrative. The foundation for her entire life was constructed mainly by her parents' words. Unfortunately, the same is true for Brianna.

THE PROGRAM IS WRITTEN

Like a brand-new computer void of programs, a newborn enters this world with only his/her personality, and no knowledge. The moment their eyes, ears, noses, mouths, and hands begin to receive messages from their environment, they start learning. According to the Center on the Developing Child at Harvard University, during the first few years of life, a million neural connections are made in the brain each second. Thus, everything that a child sees, hears, smells, touches and tastes creates a connection in their brain that is likely to last a lifetime. The connections that are made are either ***solidified*** by repetition, or ***pruned*** if the action is not continued. If the child's experience is positive, as in Jennifer's case, a strong foundation is established for a life of cognitive, emotional, and social well-being.

The meals prepared by Jennifer's mother, and the conversations that took place at the table, all contributed to the subconscious program that she was valuable and that she was loved. Each time her father showed up at one of her recitals, the narrative written on her young mind was that he was trustworthy, a man of his word. This is important on so many levels. Not only will she grow up with a healthy dose of self-worth, but she will also have a very high standard for the man she chooses to marry. The affirming words spoken over her like precious, *pretty*, *smart*, *brilliant*, and *gifted*, these words were infused into her belief system. She never had to wonder if she was brilliant, it was written on her program.

The unfortunate antithesis is that Brianna's foundation is as weak as Jennifer's is strong. Her parents failed to provide her with the nurturing that is required to create healthy connections in the brain. It's as if she was starved during her developmental stage, and every area of her life will likely be a struggle. Because her parents never took the time to listen to her, the narrative written on her young mind is that her voice doesn't matter. The prolonged stress she experienced from her parents' constant yelling and fighting had a detrimental effect on her overall health. "Toxic stress weakens the architecture of the developing brain, which can lead to lifelong problems in learning, behavior, and physical and mental health."[1]

If you have children under eight years of age, I cannot impress upon you enough that everything that happens to that little person will *matter* for the rest of their lives. It is my recommendation that you make whatever sacrifices necessary for you to give them your undivided attention. Keep in mind that, whether you actively participate in the process or not, the program *will* be written on your child's subconscious mind. This program will ultimately determine their ability to successfully navigate life. It will determine how well, or how poorly they perform in school. It will determine whether they will possess the tools to maintain a healthy, loving relationship. It will establish their belief system, their earning potential and even their physical health. My question to you, Mom and Dad, is this: will you leave it to social media, peers, teachers, babysitters, and strangers to write the program for

---

[1] https://developingchild.harvard.edu/science/key-concepts/brain-architecture/

your child? Or will you courageously and intentionally be the one to determine what kind of person your child will become?

MY SUBCONSCIOUS PROGRAM

I was born in 1963 and grew up watching television shows like *The Partridge Family*, *The Brady Bunch*, *Bewitched*, *I Dream of Jeannie*, *I Love Lucy*, *The Carol Burnett Show*, and *Charlie's Angels*. One thing that all those shows had in common was that they hardly ever included someone that looked like me. The message was clear, that all the beautiful women were white and had long hair. Since I was far from white, and my hair was short and kinky, the reflection I saw in the mirror was always a disappointment. There was a consensus among my parents, teachers, and peers that I was smart. I had no problem believing them because I had plenty of evidence to back it up. But in those days, the definition of beauty in the media did not include dark skin and kinky hair, so I leaned on my intellect and accepted the fact that I would never be considered "beautiful."

That message was solidified in my mind by my peers who always seemed to prefer the girl with the lighter skin and long, wavy hair. It didn't matter that my mother told me I was pretty. I didn't believe her because there were too many sources that contradicted her opinion. I suffered from low self-esteem, and I was unable to see my own beauty until I was thirty-eight years old. Because of the negative image I had of myself, I became promiscuous in my early teens, confusing sex with love. I felt lucky when someone wanted to marry me. Rather than making an informed decision, I jumped at the first proposal.

As a young girl, I vividly remember the little purple, velvet bags with a golden thread that my father brought home. They contained his favorite drink, Crown Royal whiskey. I would ask my dad if I could use the bags to store my doll's clothing, marbles, jacks, hair barrettes, or any random item small enough for them to hold.

In my six-year-old mind, there was something cool about those little bags. I thought they were pretty. And the fact that my dad gave them to me made them special. I watched him pour himself a drink practically every evening, and that was normal to me. Since my father was my hero, drinking the liquid that came with those pretty little purple bags had to be a good thing, right? There were even times when he would leave his drink sitting on the coffee table and, when he wasn't looking, I would take a sip. The narrative written on my young mind was that drinking alcohol was something that cool people did. And of course, I wanted to be cool.

In hindsight, I have been able to clearly define my own sub-conscious program and take the necessary steps to erase and replace it. That process enabled me to understand why I made the choices that I did in my youth, to forgive that young girl, and to heal from the trauma caused by those choices. No longer haunted by my past mistakes, I am free to enjoy the present moment, and confidently envision a successful future.

> *"Until we make the unconscious conscious, it will direct our lives and we will call it fate."*
> —CARL G. JUNG

TAKE ACTION:
IDENTIFY AND REWRITE YOUR PROGRAM

Take a deep dive into your past and see if you can determine what is included in your subconscious program. How did your parents interact with you? Were you abused or neglected? Did they allow you to use your voice, or were you told to "shut up?" Did they spend quality time with you? Or were you a latchkey kid. Looking back and evaluating how you were programmed to think is a powerful tool you can use to identify your core beliefs. You will be able to find the "why" behind many of your actions, and you will also have the power to change those beliefs if they do not serve you.

Take as much time as you need to answer the following questions candidly and honestly. Write down your answers.

1. What is it that you have always believed about yourself?
2. Can you identify the source of those beliefs?
3. Are those beliefs valid?

Once you have identified your limiting beliefs, you can move toward erasing and replacing them. But you cannot do it all at once. Just work on one thing at a time. With patience, consistency, self-discipline, and determination, you will be able to change the trajectory of your life.

Here are some suggestions to get you moving in the right direction:

Buy a Journal. Make a list of the limiting beliefs you've identified. On a different page, write down exactly what those beliefs ***should be***. Make sure you use positive, present-tense statements such as "I am," "I have," or "I can." Never say what you "don't want." Fold the page with the first list and only read it as a reference for future exercises. Read the second list aloud at least twice each day (upon waking and just before going to bed). If you are able, make a recording of this list, and listen to them while you sleep. After a few days, you should have the list memorized. You can call it your newly defined "Core Beliefs/Values" or "Affirmations." But whatever you call it, use it as your guide to the destination that you desire. Wield it like a weapon. Repetition is the key to lasting change. Because faith comes by hearing, the more you read and repeat your beliefs, the more real they will become to you. And you will be that much closer to becoming the person you truly desire to be.

> *"As you sow in your subconscious mind, so shall you reap in your body and environment."*
> —Joseph Murphy

Chapter Two

I AM

"Words are seeds that do more than blow around. They land in our hearts and not the ground. Be careful what you plant and careful what you say. You might have to eat what you planted one day."
—AUTHOR UNKNOWN

One of the most **un**true statements I learned as a child was *"sticks and stones may break my bones, but words will never hurt me."* I understand that it was meant to keep us from allowing the words spoken by others to hold too much weight in our minds. However, it is a person's own words that have the potential to create or destroy. Words spoken by an individual contain the power of life and death (Proverbs 18:21). This principle is not limited to the Bible.

Every major world religion teaches the importance of the words we speak. In Islam, the Quran emphasizes the significance of speech and the responsibility that comes with it. In Judaism, the creative power of words is deeply rooted in the belief in the power of prayer. Jews believe that God created the world through speech, and that prayers affect reality.

In Hinduism, the creative power of words is evident in the belief in mantras, sacred sounds, or phrases with transformative qualities. Right speech is one aspect of the *Noble Eightfold Path* taught in Buddhism.

One of the most powerful phrases in the English language is "I am." When those words are spoken, whatever follows them will become your reality, whether positive or negative. This phrase has a rich history that begins with the Creator Himself. When Moses asked God his name in Exodus 3:14, His response was *"I am that I am . . . tell them 'I Am' has sent you."* We were created by "I am," made in the image of "I am," and we possess the same creative power as "I am." When the words "I am" are spoken, they are supported by the power of creation! Hence, the importance of carefully crafting whatever follows that phrase.

Speaking the words *"I am so confused"* only brings more confusion. *"I am so frustrated"* only brings more frustration. *"I am so clumsy . . . stupid . . . scared"* only solidifies that reality in your mind and in your experiences.

In order for us to exercise the power that we all possess to be the arbiter of our fate, we must learn to speak only what we desire and not what our senses are telling us. To fully understand this *power*, we must first understand who we are as offspring of the Great I Am.

MADE IN HIS IMAGE

The statement "God created man in His image . . ." found in Genesis 1:27, does not mean that God looks like we do. He is not an old white man with a long grey beard (as Michelangelo would have us believe). "Image" is not referring to the way He looks. It denotes certain qualities or attributes that reflect His nature and character. Qualities such as consciousness, moral capacity, rationality, and free will. God is not a man—He is a Spirit. God is everywhere, in every place, all at the same time. He is consciousness, He is goodness and love, He is infinite intelligence and complete wisdom. And the part of us that *is* God is conscious awareness, goodness, love, intelligence, and wisdom. We innately know right from wrong because our conscience is the voice of God on the inside. It is the "light" the ignites every man that comes into the world.

Another way in which we are like God is that our words have creative power. You will find the phrase "and God said . . ." ten times in the creation story. God spoke the world into existence. He said, "Let there be . . .", and there was! Like God, we also create with our words, both intentionally and unknowingly. It's unfortunate that many people are unaware of the power of their words. They fail to understand that they are the creators of their circumstances. Like Brianna's mother, many are unhappy with their condition in life, but they place the blame on the system, their spouse, a lack of education, or their parents. They make excuses for what they've been unable to achieve, rather than taking responsibility for their own part in creating their circumstances.

My dear friend, I hate to break it to you, but the choices that you have made throughout your life brought you to this place at this moment. If you are unhappy with it, first take responsibility for your position. Then, begin to exercise the power you possess to change it!

"As a man thinketh in his heart, so is he."
—King Solomon

We cannot fully discuss the power of words without mentioning their source—thoughts.

Every word we speak begins as a thought. So, before you can control your words, you must develop the habit of confronting your thoughts. I use the term *confronting* and not *controlling*, because that would be impossible. Every day, thousands of thoughts run through our minds, many of them unwanted and intrusive. And although we cannot stop the thoughts from coming, we can decide what to do with them.

Apostle Paul gives us a master key to our thought life. "Finally, brothers and sisters, whatever is true, whatever is noble, whatever is right, whatever is pure, whatever is lovely, whatever is admirable—if anything is excellent or praiseworthy—think about such things." By focusing on what is true, we will be able to recognize a lie when we hear one. Focusing on what is noble will build nobility, high moral principles into our character. By focusing on what is right, we will not tolerate wrong. Keeping our minds pure helps ward off unnatural impulses and negative emotions. A pure mind is calm, alert, and focused. Thinking on what is lovely, admirable, and praiseworthy, we cultivate the habit of positivity. Developing the discipline of healthy thinking keeps us from be overwhelmed by our "inner critic."

THE IMPORTANCE OF SELF-TALK

If you saw someone walking down the street, talking to themselves, you would probably think they were suffering from mental illness. But the only difference between that person and you, is that they do it out loud. Most of us have a constant dialogue running through our minds every waking hour. However, problems arise when we become fused with our thoughts and accept them as truth. Just because a thought enters your mind does not mean it is valid. Just because a thought enters your mind does not mean you have to agree with it.

Many of us are constantly under "attack" by the voice in our heads. "That was so stupid! Why did you do that?" "You look so fat!" "Why even go to the party, nobody will want to talk to you!" "You can't seem to do anything right!"

"You're never going to find true love." If we spoke to our friends and family the way we speak to ourselves, we would be miserable and alone. These types of thoughts are quite common, but very counterproductive. Don't allow your thoughts to become your beliefs. We must develop the habit of separating ourselves from our thoughts and observing them. Eckhart Tolle refers to it as "watching the thinker."

When negative thoughts arise in your mind, don't just accept them. Observe them. Recognize patterns, and then confront them. When the thoughts are not in alignment with your newly defined core values, whatever you do, DO NOT give voice to them. Remember, there is creative power in words. Simply allow the thoughts to come and go, without judgment. Whatever you do, don't allow yourself to feel guilty for having a negative thought. Just replace it as you repeat out loud what you know to be true. After a short time, you will notice the thoughts coming and going, but they will not take root. They will no longer dictate your emotional state.

When your inner critic gets out of control, that's a good time to use your words as a weapon. Look on your newly defined list of governing values and beliefs for the antidote to the negative thoughts. Repeat them out loud. Remember, repetition is the key to lasting change. Repetition is the key to lasting change.

Another effective method for dealing with negative thoughts is to make a gratitude list. You can write it on your white board as a reminder throughout the day. I like to do it mentally when I wake up in the morning. Before getting out of bed, I think of all the things I'm thankful for like good health, my wonderful career, and my amazing sons. I start with the small things like how thankful I am to have a warm bed and soft pillow. I literally say these things out loud, to feel the full effect of the gratitude.

When you are in an active state of gratitude, focusing on what you are thankful for and saying it out loud, your brain releases the *feel-good* chemicals—serotonin and dopamine. Staying in an attitude of gratitude not only stops the inner critic from taking over, but it also aids in alleviating depression and anxiety.

"Watch your thoughts, they become your words;
watch your words, they become your actions;
watch your actions, they become your habits;
watch your habits, they become your character;
watch your character, it becomes your destiny."

—LAO TZU

Chapter Three

LOVE VS. FEAR

*Love is patient, love is kind, it is not jealous; love
does not brag, it is not arrogant. It does not act
disgracefully, it does not seek its own benefit;
it is not provoked, does not keep an account of a
wrong suffered, it does not rejoice in
unrighteousness, but rejoices with the truth; it
keeps every confidence, it believes all things, hopes
all things, endures all things. Love never fails.*
—APOSTLE PAUL

Love is a skill set that must be developed and strengthened.
It contains the attributes mentioned in the above quote by
Apostle Paul: patience, kindness, selflessness, humility,
compassion, hope, and endurance. Although love is not

necessarily a feeling, your body does experience the *sensations* that come with the release of neurotransmitters in the brain when you are attracted to someone. In fact, all feelings and emotions are a result of chemical reactions in your body. Dopamine and oxytocin are often referred to as the *Love Chemicals*. The other "feel good" chemicals are serotonin and endorphins. These hormones are not only responsible for the feeling of attraction, but they also have several physiological functions. They contribute to relieving pain, reducing stress, regulating mood, establishing sleep patterns, and creating an overall sense of well-being.

Acts of charity also cause these "happiness hormones" to be released, which is why we feel so good when we give to those in need. Studies have shown that giving to others makes you happier than buying for yourself. Oxytocin is also released during childbirth and breastfeeding, creating that unique, mother and child bond.

Even though we are surrounded by negativity, our true nature is love. We were created by Love, made in the image of Love, and we possess the power of Love. However, we cannot begin to experience true harmony until we are in alignment with this principle. The Creator's intention for mankind was for us to dwell in love and allow it to be the motivation for everything we do. The reason it is more blessed to give than to receive is because encoded in our DNA is the need to care for, support, and help one another. True fulfillment comes from doing what we were created to do—to love.

As far back as I can remember, I heard the phrase "God is Love." I knew my parents loved me, and I knew that Jesus loved me, "for the Bible tells me so." But an entire lifetime passed before I was able to grasp the concept of real *love* and encounter it in its fullness.

My parents were divorced when I reached the age of nine, so my foundation was shaken, and my understanding of love was skewed. Movies and television portrayed love as a physical, sensual experience. Therefore, as a young teen, I mistook sex for love. And when I first married my husband, I thought our love (attraction) for one another was enough to sustain a life of happiness and fulfillment. But what I labeled "falling in love" was actually the dopamine rush that took place in my brain whenever I saw him. I couldn't possibly have been **in love** because I had not yet learned to love myself.

SELF-LOVE

Loving yourself does not mean that you feel warm and fuzzy every time you look in the mirror. It does, however, mean that when you see your own image, you think and feel positively about what you see. For far too long, I was unhappy with my physical appearance, and that fact alone made it difficult for me to love myself. I would always have thoughts like "If only my nose were thinner" or "I wish my hair was longer." I was so busy focusing on what I believed were my flaws that I couldn't see the incredible person I was in the process of becoming. I was confident in my musical talent and my intellect. But I still felt like I had to prove myself to be worthy of love . . . even my own love.

Loving myself means seeing value in **who I am**, regardless of my appearance or my accomplishments. For most of my life, I believed that my performance made me valuable. Getting good grades, scoring the highest on tests, winning competitions and being the BEST in every possible way. Those are the things that made me feel worthy of love, for a while. Until I reached a season in my life where everything felt like a constant battle, and I failed consistently. Then I was unable to see my value.

Between 1984 and 1989 I struggled with drug addiction. During this period, I felt absolutely worthless. The only thing that kept me from going under was the fact that I was responsible for three little lives. Motherhood saved my life. The intensity of the love that I felt for those little guys was unlike anything I'd ever known.

One day, as I was playing with my boys, the thought entered my mind that God had entrusted *me* with the care of these amazing little beings. He must have known something about me that I had yet to learn. Not only did He *trust* me, but He also loved me. I felt God's love through my babies. Those three little gifts showered me with so much unconditional love, it made me want to live a life deserving of that love. My understanding of the nature of love continued to grow as I experienced God's love throughout my addiction. There were many times when I felt like an absolute failure. It's during those time that I felt the most connected to God. His love was tangible.

One of the many examples of God's tangible love took place in 1997. I had just finished a three-day binge during which my aunt Malinda took care of my babies. The dope house was only three blocks away, but the walk back home to Malinda and my sons felt more like a thousand mile walk of shame! I didn't know how I was going to face her after my disappearing act. I totally expected her to be furious and yell at me. But she was so happy to see me. She just hugged me and cried. She told me that I was already forgiven and allowed me to sleep while she kept the boys for another twenty-four hours. When I awoke the next afternoon, my babies were waiting to throw their little arms around me and shower me with love and affection.

"We missed you Mommy," Davion said as they all jumped in my lap and threw their little arms around my neck.

In that moment I felt completely unlovable, but that didn't stop them from loving me! They were totally unaware of what I had just done. Even if they knew, it wouldn't matter. Their love for me was unconditional, just like God's. That afternoon, I sat down at the piano and began to pour my heart out to him.

"I'll never know why, why you did what you did. You didn't have to die, but you did. You hung on the cross so that I wouldn't be lost. You took my place, now you're pleading my case. You didn't have to do it, oh but I'm glad you did. You didn't have to do it, but I'm glad you did."

Not long after this, I received a call from a producer friend of mine. He was looking for songs for an artist by the name of Crystal Lewis. Before I knew it, we were in the studio recording *You Didn't Have to Do It*. The entire time, I was in awe of what was happening. It didn't matter that I was still addicted to crack cocaine, and that I had just finished a three-day binge. God still chose to pour this song into my soul and then allow it to be recorded almost immediately. It eventually became one of her biggest hits.

I experienced the tangible love of God through my children. His forgiveness through my Aunt Malinda, and His beautiful gift through my music. No matter how many times I had fallen, God continued to shine His light through me and cover me with His love. That was reason enough for me to love myself. The more I learn to love myself, the less I need to seek love from outside myself. However, on my journey of self-discovery, self-improvement, and self-love, there was another force at work.

"Deep down, at our cores, there are only two emotions: love and fear."
—ELISABETH KUBLER-ROSS

In chapter one, I discussed how my young mind was programmed to see drugs and alcohol as a normal part of life. Another aspect of my sub-conscious programming took place as a result of my parents' divorce. Up until the age of nine, I saw my life as perfect. I had two perfect parents and two cool older brothers. I had my own bedroom in a beautiful home in the city of Inglewood and a German Shepherd named Buddy. Life was beautiful and I felt safe and happy. When my parents' marriage failed, however, everything changed. It was as if the bottom fell out of my life and my security went with it.

My father moved out and we were forced to leave our beautiful home and move into an apartment. We ultimately moved from one apartment to another each year, over the course of the next ten years. We went from 9801 S. Van Ness, to the Aku Aku apartments on 104th and Doty. Then to an apartment in The Jungle on August Street, to The Watergate apartments near Wilshire and Normandie. From there it was Pico and West Blvd, to The University apartments on Vermont and Jefferson. My dad purchased a house in Van Nuys, and we lived with him for a brief period, then back to an apartment in Inglewood on Venice Way and Beach Ave. We lived with my mother's friend,

Denise, for a few months. Then, my father purchased a tiny house on 60th and 7th Ave, and Anthony and I moved in with him. That's where I spent the next three years while I attended Crenshaw High School.

When my parents were together, life was beautiful. Money never seemed to be an issue, at least not one that I was aware of. After my parents separated, the struggle to make ends meet became a way of life for us. Not just for my mother but for my father as well. Together, they seemed to be successful. But apart, life was a constant battle. One of my father's favorite sayings was "I got $20 to last until payday." Financial hardship was all I knew, and it became my reality for many years.

The experience of constantly being uprooted and shuffling from one place to another created a set of beliefs in my subconscious mind. I believed that I could never be successful as a single woman, that I had to be married to experience financial security and stability. Also, the experience of watching both my parents struggle financially developed within me a strong case of *fear of Lack*. It was from this place of fear that I interacted with the world around me. Beneath all my hard work was the fear that I would never have enough. I was consumed by this constant dread, but completely unaware of it. It had become my "normal."

My situation is not unique. Millions of people are consumed by fear. Fear of public speaking, fear of spiders, fear of heights, fear of enclosed spaces, fear of going outside, fear of crowds, fear of success, fear of failure, fear of death and fear of the unknown, just to name a few.

> *"There is no fear in love. But perfect love drives out fear because fear has to do with punishment. The one who fears is not made perfect in love."*
> —APOSTLE JOHN

It's important to understand that **love** and **fear** are equally powerful forces. They operate in ways that are quite similar but have opposite effects. Both fear and love are contagious and have the power to shape the collective consciousness. They both require faith. Fear is simply faith in the worst possible outcome. Love hopes for the best. Fear reacts. Love responds. Fear paralyzes. Love moves us forward. Fear results in selfishness, jealousy, insecurity, stress, anxiety, hatred, and anger. Love brings us to a place of joy, confidence, compassion, and peace.

Love and fear are like two sides of the same coin, but they cannot work together. If you throw a quarter in the air, it will land on either heads, or tails. It will never be both. In the same way, you are always operating under the influence of *either* love *or* fear. And every day, you are faced with a choice between the two.

When someone tells us something about ourselves that we don't want to hear, fear will react, deflect, and become defensive and angry. Love will listen without judgement, accept what is true and be grateful for the opportunity to grow. When we are in a position to help someone in need, fear will hold back what should be freely given. Love will make a sacrifice and give.

To reach and maintain a place of inner harmony, you must return to your core, which is love. Allow love to be the motivation behind all that you do, which begins with loving yourself. Let patience, kindness, selflessness, humility, compassion, hope, and endurance be your strong foundation.

> *"Love is what happens when we stop trying to figure out who deserves it."*
>
> —KAREN FAITH

On your journey of self-love, forgive your past mistakes. Keep in mind that you *cannot* change the past. Be grateful for **everything** that took place in your life which brought you to this moment and made you who you are. Accept your flaws, your humanity. Stop expecting perfection. When the voice in your head begins its attack, reminding you of all that's wrong about you, take a moment and repeat these words to yourself, *"I am worthy of love. I was created by love, made in the image of love, and the power of love dwells in me."*

> *"You can conquer almost any fear if you will only*
> *make up your mind to do so. For remember,*
> *fear doesn't exist anywhere except in the mind."*
> —DALE CARNEGIE

Chapter Four

ACCEPTANCE

"Accept the rain as easily as you accept the sunshine. Both are necessary for growth."
—Jackie Gouche

Vicky and Greg were married when they were both only twenty-three. After the wedding, Greg wasn't as affectionate as he had been during their courtship. Despite his lack of intimacy, they welcomed a son, Conner, after two years of marriage. Greg was ecstatic at being a new father, especially since he had a boy. He would take his son everywhere. He spent so much time with his baby boy that Vicky began to feel neglected. She thought maybe she was being selfish and didn't express her feelings to Greg. *He's just being a good father*, she thought.

Five years passed before Vicky became pregnant with their second child. On her way to give Greg the good news, he announced that he had some news of his own. He told his wife that he would be filing for divorce. But the news didn't end there. He was leaving her for Jonathan. Vicky was devastated!

Michelle and Stephen met in college and got married during their senior year. A few months into the marriage, Stephen began to feel like he'd made a mistake. All his friends were just beginning to discover themselves. They were dating, partying, and having fun while Stephen was going home to his wife. Even though he felt like he missed out on a part of life, he didn't want to hurt Michelle. So, he committed to stay in the relationship, hoping that his feelings would change. They had two boys and a girl.

Stephen struggled with feelings of dissatisfaction and frustration over the next sixteen years but kept his feelings well-hidden for the children's sake. From everyone else's perspective, Stephen and Michelle had a beautiful family and a happy marriage. But Stephen lived with a constant ache in his heart.

When he could no longer deal with the void, he began to fill it with occasional, meaningless sex with random women. The first few times if felt good. But after a while it began to make the void in his heart expand. No longer able to live with his secrets, Stephen told Michelle how he felt and what he'd done. Then told her that, after eighteen years of what she thought was a perfect marriage, he wanted a divorce.

Michelle was devastated!

Both Vicky and Michelle will tell you that divorce is hard. But only Vicky can tell you how to heal from the pain and move on. She reached out to her family and her spiritual community for support and immediately began seeing a therapist. It wasn't an easy road. There were many, many tears, but Vicky, Greg and Jonathan were able to establish a peaceful, co-parenting relationship. Five years after the divorce, they were all good friends.

Five years after her divorce, Michelle still goes straight to the bar after work every day, trying to find the reason her marriage ended.

Acceptance means allowing unpleasant experiences to exist without denying, hiding from, or trying to change them. It is what it is. That may sound trite, but if something is completely out of your control, and there's nothing you can do to change it, then . . . it is what it is. Accept that.

Live with the pain until it's no longer painful. Find someone who can sit with you in the pain and help you navigate your way out of it. As long as we are human, pain is inevitable. It's a part of life. Attempting to live a life without pain is to deny reality. Acceptance allows us to make peace with the things we cannot change, and to go *through* the pain instead of wallowing in it.

The moment Vicky was hit with the news of her husband's same-sex attraction, the ache in her heart was so severe, she didn't know how she was going to make it through the next hour, let alone how she was going to live the rest of her life. But even amid her tears, she realized that this situation was completely out of her control. She had no choice but to accept it, forgive her husband and begin healing.

Michelle refused to accept that the man she'd loved since college never loved her the way she believed he had. She couldn't face the fact that it was over after eighteen beautiful years.

She would ask herself daily, *"Why didn't I know? How could I not know?"* Her failed marriage became the topic of conversation with any and everyone. Her friends and family tried to help her to move on. But after a few years, many of them concluded that she would never let go, so they began to distance themselves from her. Even her children were unable to help their mother get over the break-up, and they couldn't stand to watch her suffer any longer, so they chose to go out of state for college.

Michelle didn't make the conscious choice to wallow in her pain. She just never accepted the reality of her situation and lived the rest of her life in the bitterness of *"I can't believe he did that to me."*

> *"Things work out best for those who make the best of how things work out."*
> —John Wooden

SELF-ACCEPTANCE

In the world of psychology, there are many issues surrounding the "self." Self-esteem, self-compassion, self-worth, self-care, self-love, self-awareness, and self-actualization. But at the root of all these practices is self-acceptance. You cannot begin to exercise self-anything until you first accept yourself for who you are. It simply means embracing every part of you, not just the good parts.

"True self-acceptance is embracing who you are, without any qualifications, conditions, or exceptions."[2] Because we are so multi-faceted and constantly changing, embracing who we are is a life-long process.

I was blessed with the thickest, kinkiest 4-C hair one can imagine. Unfortunately, to me it felt more like a curse. As far back as I can remember, I would sit on the floor in front of someone and listen to them complain as they yanked my head back and forth, ignoring my cries of pain. When I wasn't on the floor being tortured, I was sitting at the kitchen table. I'd watched as the straightening come got hotter and hotter, praying that I wouldn't get burned on my ear or the back of my neck. I wish I could say I had a love/hate relationship with my hair, but it was only hate. I was programmed to see my hair as a problem that needed to be solved.

I permed (chemically straightened) my hair when was in the sixth grade. That didn't turn out well at all. In 1975, the Jheri-curl swooped in and rescued me from the daily dilemma growing from my scalp. That relationship lasted until I was twenty-one. That's when I discovered weaves.

---

2 Seltzer, L. F. (2008). The path to unconditional self-acceptance. Psychology Today. Retrieved from https://www.psychologytoday.com/us/blog/evolution-the-self/200809/the-path-unconditional-self-acceptance

For the next forty years, no one saw my real hair. I went from weaves, to braids, to wigs and back to weaves. Every now and then I would let someone press my hair, just to see if it was long enough to make me cute. It never grew past my shoulders.

Over the years, I've gradually accepted aspects of who I am. When I reached the age of thirty-eight, I looked in the mirror and finally saw a beautiful woman. I accepted my nose after hating it for most of my life. I embraced my dark skin and my thick thighs. I accepted my weaknesses, mistakes, flaws, and limitations. I accepted everything but my hair. That didn't happen until I turned fifty-nine. I finally stopped putting other people's hair on my head and began a loving relationship with my own.

Today, there is nothing about me that I don't love. When we accept ourselves fully and unconditionally, we no longer need validation or approval from others.

> *Whatever the present moment contains, accept it as if you had chosen it. Always work with it, not against it".*
> —ECKHART TOLLE

ACCEPT YOUR CIRCUMSTANCES

Life is filled with the unexpected. Both Vicky and Michelle were blindsided when their marriages failed. But their responses took them down two completely different paths. They were faced with the choice between love and fear. Vicky chose the path of love. She started by forgiving Greg, releasing herself from the anger and resentment that was otherwise inevitable. She put her ego aside and thought about the years he spent denying his true identity, and how difficult that must have been for him. She exercised one of the characteristics found in Apostle Paul's definition of love—selflessness. On her healing journey, Vicky put herself in her ex-husband's shoes, and had compassion for him.

Michelle was in denial until the day the divorce was final. The thought never crossed her mind to consider how her ex-husband must have felt. She was unable to exercise selflessness because she had chosen the path of fear. She was afraid that she would be alone for the rest of her life, and that she would never be loved. Michelle was afraid that her best years were behind her. She got stuck in a loop of pain and resentment and the thing she feared the most came upon her. No one was willing to attend her pity party.

She died of cancer seven years after her divorce, never having experience true love.

Acceptance is the master-key to peace. By allowing things to be as they are, you eliminate the inner turmoil that comes with fighting reality. Consciously choosing the path of love and compassion will empower you to overcome your challenges, and to grow as a result.

> *"The youth can walk faster,*
> *but the elder knows the road."*
> —African Proverb

ACCEPT AGING

When I was eleven years old, the thought never occurred to me that I would one day die. I felt invincible. Even when I flipped over on the last hump of the giant slide, and broke my leg, I didn't consider the fact that it could have been tragic. I could have broken my neck and become paralyzed, or worse. I could have died. I was given a cast from my thigh to my ankle, and I wore it with pride. My friends signed it, and I would get a kick out of the funny things some of them wrote. I had absolutely no worries, I knew that my leg would heal.

Today, at sixty, thoughts of my mortality come often. Because of the prolonged stress of my drug days, I developed arthritis. I was diagnosed at age fifty and had surgery on my right knee.

"No more running," my doctor said.

"For how long?" I replied.

"No more running . . . period." I couldn't believe what I was hearing. His words made no sense to me. No more running . . . ever?? How could that be? How was I supposed to live the rest of my life without running? Not willing to believe that I would never run again, I ignored his orders and tried to run anyway. The pain I experienced afterward convinced me that I should listen to my doctor.

At first, my brain wasn't willing to accept the reality of my condition. I'd spent the entire decade of my forties in the gym, squatting, lunging, running, jumping, and lifting weights. I was in the best physical shape of my life. Then, suddenly, everything was different. I went through a period of depression over the next few years, focusing on what I **couldn't** do.

I eventually grew tired of feeling bad and began to change my focus. I went back to school and was reminded how much I love learning. Building my brain became more important to me that building my body. It was changing, and I had to accept that. I thought about all my peers, friends from high school who were no longer with us; colleagues from the music industry who had passed on, many of whom were younger than me. I decided to be thankful for my life, such as it was.

Western culture has done a great disservice to the world by promoting the goal of being "forever young." We desperately fight the aging process with creams, potions, surgery, and make-up. The lines around our eyes, and the sagging jowls make us feel as if we are losing our value. Now eighty-three, my mother lives in an assisted living facility. I visit her several times each week and can't help but notice the loneliness of many of the other people living there. No one ever comes to visit them. They sit in their wheelchairs in the lobby, hallways and tv room, often with a blank stare on their faces. My heart aches for them.

Aging is a matter of perspective. When I'm visiting my mother, although I am sixty years old, I feel like a young person. When I'm enjoying the company of my girlfriends, I still feel like a teenager. When I'm with my grandchildren, instead of feeling old, I relish the wisdom that I'm able to share with them. I may not be able to run, but I can walk with the sun's rays beaming down on my face, fresh air in my lungs and an attitude of gratitude.

> *"God, grant me the serenity to accept the things*
> *I cannot change, courage to change the things*
> *I can and wisdom to know the difference".*
> —REINHOLD NIEBUHR

Chapter Five

PERSPECTIVE

"When I look at me, the only thing
I see is what the mirror says to me.
But when You look at me, You see everything
You had in mind when You created me.
I see all my flaws, all my blemishes and wrinkles.
But You see all the beauty that You placed inside
of me. If only I could see the way you see . . ."
—Jackie Gouché

Perspective is the lens through which you see the world. Like fingerprints, everyone's perspective is uniquely their own. Many conflicts arise in relationships because one or both parties fail to see the situation from the other's perspective. Take Vicky and Michelle, for example. Even with a broken heart, Vicky was able to stop focusing on her own pain and consider the situation from her husband's perspective. She thought about the fact that he sincerely tried to do what he believed was right. Greg was raised in the church, so he was "supposed" to fall in love with a woman, get married and start a family. He had to suppress his true desires and deny what was in his heart. He lived a conflicted, painful life. It was Vicky's consideration of Greg's pain that caused her to have compassion and forgive him. This is a sign of true, emotional maturity.

Michelle didn't even attempt to see things from anyone's perspective but her own. She was the victim. Her husband cheated on her. He ended their *perfect* marriage. Of course, she perceived the marriage as perfect because she was only looking at it from her own perspective. It never occurred to her that Stephen had suppressed his true feelings, and lived eighteen years in frustration and regret, yet still managed to make her feel loved **and** be a good father. I know, that's not the ideal situation, but it is reality. A reality that was lost on Michelle. All she could see was that he cheated on her and broke her heart. Focusing daily on her pain prevented her from ever healing and moving on. Her perspective was that of a victim.

Although Vicky felt the pain of the divorce, she saw herself as the arbiter of **her** own destiny. She understood that it was her choices that would determine her outcome, not her husband's.

You can change your entire life by changing your perspective. And not just your future, you can re-frame your past in such a way that it changes the effect it had on you. I'll explain what I mean.

My husband was incarcerated for nearly seven years, leaving me alone to raise three baby boys. They were one, two, and three when he went in and eight, nine and ten when he came home. Although I forgave him and we stayed together, for many years I carried a molecule of anger and resentment for having been left alone. It was always there under the surface, like a splinter under my fingernail. Until just a few years ago, when I had a conversation with my cousin, Sheila, on the topic of Ronald's incarceration. For a moment I was reminded of my splinter, until Sheila said this:

"That was the best thing that could've happened. Those babies had you all to themselves, and you had their undivided attention. You were able to pour yourself, and all your musical knowledge into those boys while they were developing. If

Ronald had been there, everything would have been different. They wouldn't be who they are! They would have grown up to be different people! It happened exactly as it was supposed to happen!"

As soon as I heard her words, the splinter began to dissolve. I was immediately able to see the good in what I had always framed as a bad situation. I literally cried as I thought of the truth of her words, and how many years I wasted feeling angry. From that day forward, I no longer carried the pain of being a single mother. Another thing that happened in my conversation with my cousin was that my regret suddenly turned to gratitude! Now when I think about the time I spent raising my sons alone, I do it with a smile. My newfound perspective of the past changed my present and future experiences.

Each of us has the power to choose our perspective. When you're stuck in traffic, you can decide to allow it to send you into your default mode of frustration, irritation, and anxiety. Or you can choose a positive mindset. Take advantage of the extra time by putting on a good audiobook, motivational podcast, or soothing music. Creating an atmosphere of *chill mode* in your car is so much healthier than being angry at the other drivers. Accept the fact that you will always have to share the road, leave early to give yourself plenty of travel time and don't allow traffic to dictate your emotional state. You are in the driver's seat, literally and figuratively.

> *"We see the world not as it is, but as we are."*
> —Stephen Covey

The way you experience life depends largely on the how see yourself. A good example of this is a man named Nick Vujicic. Nick was born with no arms or legs, but he is a warm, loving, kind, inspirational man with a positive perspective. He's an author, he runs a non-profit organization, he has a beautiful wife and four biological children. After going through a deep depression between age eight and twelve, he finally made the choice to "be thankful for what I have instead of being angry for what I don't have." He used the power of choice to change his perspective, thereby changing his life. Rather than focusing on his limitations, he chooses to focus on the possibilities.

Nick could have chosen to see himself as a victim. He had every reason to spend his life feeling sad and depressed because of his disability. Instead, he chose to **accept** the things he would never be able to do, and to push the limits and find out that he *was* able to do. Nick may not have arms or legs, but he plays golf, swims, and surfs. He also travels the world sharing the message that he lives his life with an attitude of gratitude.

> *"If in this life only we have hope in Christ, we are of all men most miserable."*
>
> —Apostle Paul

ETERNAL PERSPECTIVE

The major world religions, Buddhism, Christianity, Islam, Hinduism, and Judaism all believe that we continue to live in one form or another after physical death. Many also believe in the eternal nature of our souls, that we existed prior to our lives on earth. I believe that Nick Vujicic's ability to have a positive outlook on life is based on his understanding or belief that we are spiritual beings having a transient, physical experience. Although he must live his entire life without arms or legs, he finds comfort in his belief that he will continue in a perfect, spiritual form after his physical body expires.

The following excerpt from a Time Magazine article entitled *"Does Spirituality Make You Happy"* confirms the value of spiritual beliefs and practices.

"Study after study has found that religious people tend to be less depressed and less anxious than nonbelievers, better able to handle the vicissitudes of life than nonbelievers. A 2015 survey by researchers at the London School of Economics and the Erasmus University Medical Center in the Netherlands found that participating in a religious organization was the only social activity associated with sustained happiness—even more than volunteering for a charity, taking educational courses or participating in a political or community organization. It's as if a sense of spirituality and an active, social religious practice were an effective vaccine against the virus of unhappiness." [3]

NEAR DEATH EXPERIENCE

One of mankind's greatest fears is the fear of death, which is based in the fear of the unknown. To some, the idea that someone could die, and then come back to report their findings is a mere fantasy. However, in 1975 Dr. Raymond

---

[3] https://time.com/4856978/spirituality-religion-happiness/

Moody published a book called *Life After Life*, in which he "investigates more than 100 case studies of people who experienced 'clinical death' and were subsequently revived."

There are countless numbers of people who have returned from actual death, whether by resuscitation or other miraculous means. These people claim to have had an ultra-real, vivid experience of the "other side." Heart attack, drowning, electrocution, car accident, disease, and various other means of death, send these near-death-ers on a journey in which they encounter the spiritual realm. People from different cultures, beliefs, languages, and backgrounds report having similar experiences. They include leaving their bodies and watching from a different perspective as the emergency workers frantically try to resuscitate them. They describe with uncanny accuracy what was said and done while there was no brain activity, and it was supposedly impossible for them to have known. It is also very common for them to have an overwhelming sense of peace, and a feeling of being unconditionally loved.

Whether you are religious, agnostic, or even atheist, the perspective that there is more to being human than life in these physical bodies can be a powerful source of strength and hope.

Perspective

If you change the way you look at things, the things you look at change.

—Wayne Dyer

Chapter Six

THE PHYSIOLOGY OF HARMONY

"Get on the floor! Face down! Don't look at me!" he said, pointing the gun directly in my face. My legs buckled under me, and I fell down. But even before I reached the floor, my heart started beating so intensely, I felt like it was going to burst through my chest. I heard another loud voice coming from the living room.

"Tell me where the money is, or I'm gon' start shooting these bitches one by one!" he said, referring to me and my friend, Milly. My entire body was shaking uncontrollably, literally burning with fear. I thought surely, I was about to die, and that thought began to wreak havoc on my body.

"When you're scared, . . . your brain sets off an elaborate and coordinated set of responses to help you stay safe, . . . Physical changes—from deep inside your brain all the way to the muscles in your legs—happen in seconds."[4]

The scene described above was a very real, life-threatening event that I experienced during my addiction many years ago. My body immediately went into "fight or flight" mode, also referred to as the *Acute Stress response*. In a fraction of a second, my brain released the hormone, adrenaline, setting off a chain reaction. My heart rate and blood pressure increased. My breathing became quick and shallow. There was a decrease in blood flow to my pre-frontal cortex, the part of the brain responsible for logic and decision making. That blood was diverted to my major muscle groups, enabling me to run from the threat.

Because it borrows energy from the immune and digestive systems, this heightened state is not meant to last too long, hence the term *acute*.

---

4 https://rightasrain.uwmedicine.org/well/health/your-body-fear-anxiety#:~:text=Some%20people%20may%20get%20sweaty,the%20body%2C%E2%80%9D%20says%20Evans.

Unfortunately, you don't have to be held at gunpoint for this stress response to be triggered. Your body has the same reaction to financial pressure, toxic relationships, loss of a job, death of a loved one, illness, divorce, and numerous other stressors. Many people live in a state of chronic stress for several reasons, including poverty, a difficult boss or co-worker, abusive parents, or a cheating spouse. Under these conditions, everyday life can feel as stressful as being held at gunpoint. However, our bodies are not meant to live in fight or flight mode for long periods of time. It compromises our immune system, lowering our ability to fight disease.

> *"It's not stress that kills us; it is our reaction to it."*
> —HANS SELYE

HOMEOSTASIS

I have had asthma ever since I can remember. My parents would drive me to the Kaiser Hospital located on Manchester and Crenshaw, nearly every week. At each visit, the first thing they would do is take my temperature. I never understood, or even questioned why that was necessary, but let's take a moment and consider it.

To be in good health, our bodies need to maintain a state of balance, or *homeostasis*. Our temperature should hover around 98.6 degrees Fahrenheit. This baseline temperature is referred to as the set point.

A process called *thermoregulation* works to maintain this set point. Our internal thermostat causes us to sweat when we get too hot, and shiver when we get too cold. Of course, the process is infinitely more complex than that last sentence. Our bodies are constantly at work to keep us as close to the set point as possible, protecting us from either **hyper**thermia (too hot), or **hypo**thermia (too cold), both of which can be deadly.

The principle of homeostasis can also be applied to our psychological or emotional well-being. Imagine your emotional *set point* as a calm, relaxed state. Not too excited, sad, or depressed. Doing our best to remain in this "chill mode" is the emotional equivalent to thermoregulation. While our physical bodies are working to keep us at 98.6, our thoughts, words, choices, and actions are responsible for maintaining our **emotional set point**.

Too often, people allow outside stimuli to govern their emotional state. Saying someone **made** you angry, **made** you happy, **made** you sad or depressed, puts the power to determine your well-being in their hands. The physical process of thermoregulation happens automatically. But governing your emotional state is an act of your will. No one can ***make*** me anything. The choice is mine.

Homeostasis, or balance, is also required in the acid/alkaline levels in our blood. The range for measuring the blood pH level is 0-14, with 7.35 to 7.45 being the "set point." Diseases thrive in an acidic environment. Cancer thrives in an acidic environment. **Acidic emotions** include fear, hatred, jealousy, shame, depression, despair, anxiety, bitterness, resentment, and entitlement. **Alkaline emotions** are love, joy, peace, forgiveness, freedom, hope, and optimism.

Remember Michelle? She chose to allow her husband's actions to send her into a perpetual state of anger and depression, causing her to live year after year in *fight or flight* mode. This prolonged stress weakened her immune system, making her susceptible to cancer. When she received her diagnosis, she continued living in a negative, **acidic** emotional state, creating the perfect environment for the cancer to thrive. If Michelle had chosen the path of love over fear, if she had forgiven her husband and allowed herself to heal, she might still be alive today.

Chapter Seven

THE POWER OF MUSIC

"Words make you think a thought.
Music makes you feel a feeling.
A song makes you feel a thought."
—E.Y. HARBURG

Music has had an immeasurable and profound impact on my life. I grew up watching my mother play piano and sing in church and on night club stages. She also had a brief record contract, but that part of her career never got off the ground. My older brother, Andrew Gouché, carved out a significant place in the music world as a bass player. He was a pioneer, playing the bass guitar in church before it was an actual thing.

Thanks to his influence, I was also blessed to work in the field of music beginning at the age of 15. Before either of us became professionals, we simply enjoyed the sounds of soul music that constantly reverberated throughout our home.

The soundtrack to my childhood included The Jackson Five's *I Want You Back*. Aretha Franklin's many hits such as *Respect*, *Rock Steady*, and *Natural Woman*. The Temptations' *Runaway Child, Ball of Confusion*, and *My Girl*, Smokey Robinson's *Tracks of My Tears*, and dozens of other songs. What these songs all have in common is that, although it's been over fifty years since they were released, I still remember all the lyrics to each of them. Part of the reason I can remember those songs so easily is because of the number of times I heard them. I mentioned earlier the power of repetition.

My ability to remember lyrics can also be attributed to the emotional stimulation that takes place when we listen to music. Any experience connected to a strong emotion has a way of embedding itself in our long-term memory in a much greater manner than something that has no emotional element, like the stuff we were taught in fifth-grade science class. That's why most adults lost on the game show, *Smarter Than a Fifth Grader*.

I always got good grades in middle school. So, in my mother's mind I was a good little girl. She had no idea how I was spending my time. Like Brianna in chapter two, I lost my virginity at the age of thirteen. The song, 'Love Won't Let Me Wait' by Major Harris, had a lot to do with that. With lyrics about spending the night in wonderland, exploding in ecstasy, and the sounds of a woman moaning sensually throughout the song, my little pre-pubescent hormones didn't stand a chance. I listened to that song every day and imagined that I was that woman. I wondered what if felt like.

Music is one of the most powerful *influencers* known to man. It transcends time and embodies emotion. The songs we grew up listening to are all connected to our memory of the events of that day. Music has the power to transport us back in time and cause us to relive the scene set to a particular song. When I hear 'Love Won't Let Me Wait' even before he starts singing, the sound of the sultry saxophone in the intro, and the strings that accompany it, send me right back to that insecure little seventh grader who just wanted to be loved. I feel what she felt.

As I listened to that song as a thirteen-year-old, I was completely unaware of what was taking place in my brain.

The music stimulated my Limbic system, causing it to release dopamine, the same neurotransmitter that made me feel like I was "in love" when I first met my husband. So, listening to that song actually made me feel like I was in love, and of course, the result was me taking my clothes off in front of that boy.

Music can influence us individually, guiding our behavior and choices, like the effect Major Harris had on me. It can also influence society as a whole. Think about the effect Elvis and The Beatles had on an entire generation. They changed the landscape of American culture, introducing many elements that are now considered common in the music world. Throughout history, music has played a significant role in shaping cultural norms, social movements, and even political ideologies. From protest songs during the civil rights movement to anthems of unity during times of crisis, music has been a catalyst for change and a voice for the marginalized.

> *"Music gives a soul to the universe,*
> *wings to the mind, flight to the imagination,*
> *and life to everything."*
>
> —PLATO

Another powerful effect of music is that it literally *moves* us. "In some African languages, the same word means both 'music' and 'dance' because to have one without the other is simply unthinkable." [5]

In 1960, Chubby Checker sparked a worldwide phenomenon with his song 'The Twist,' that had people of all cultures, ages and backgrounds shaking their hips from side to side. This song, and many others like it have a dual effect on us. It unites us by causing us to move in sync with the beat and with one another. It also connects us emotionally. It doesn't matter what part of the world you are from. A sad song in Europe is sad in America as well. A song that evokes happiness, does so no matter where you're from. Songs like, 'I Got A Feeling' by the Black Eyed Peas and 'Happy' by Pharrell Williams, brought joy to listeners from America to Bulgaria, from Africa to Slovakia. These songs transcended culture and language and made the world dance together.

> *"Music is the medicine of the mind."*
> —JOHN LOGAN

---

5 https://www.theguardian.com/stage/theatreblog/2011/apr/06/dance-music-spoken-word

Music can also act as a cathartic release, allowing us to express and process our own feelings and experiences. When words fail to convey the depth of our emotions, music fills in the gaps, resonating with us in ways that mere speech cannot. Many hit songs become hits because of the number of people that can identify with the message of the song.

Whether we are singing along or simply listening, music allows us to connect to our emotions in ways that are both personal and universal.

In recent times, the digital age has transformed the way we consume music and the extent of its influence. Online streaming platforms and social media have made music accessible to innumerable people across the globe. It has also become a driving force in the world of marketing, influencing our behaviors and choices, from what we wear to even our political affiliations. Advertisers recognize the power of music to evoke emotions and seamlessly integrate it into their campaigns, capitalizing on its ability to capture our attention and manipulate our desires.

It's important that we recognize how we are influenced by music. It's even more important for creators of music to be aware of how they are influencing the behavior of those who listen. Take responsibility for the lyrical content, understanding that you could be the cause of a young girl losing her innocence.

SACRED MUSIC

I believe that all music is powerful, but none matches the power of sacred music. From Handel's *Messiah* to Kirk Franklin's *Now Behold the Lamb*, spiritual songs go directly into our souls, and move them in a way that is healing, and transformative. In the book of 1 Samuel, we find the account of King Saul being troubled by an evil spirit. He called for David, who was a *cunning player on the harp*. David's skillful musicianship caused the evil spirit to depart, and King Saul was refreshed. Millions of people around the world and throughout history have had a similar experience, including me. During some of the most challenging times of my life, it was a song that comforted me and gave me strength. I'm sure this is true for many people. But in my case, the song came ***through*** me. You already know about the song given to me after my cocaine binge. I received another gift a few years later.

The song, *'My Help,'* was given to me in a dream. It felt almost like déjà vu. I was at the keyboard in my church, with my band and praise team. All the familiar faces were there in the congregation, lifting their hands and singing along. *"My help . . . my help. My help, all of my help cometh from the Lord . . ."* The entire song, from beginning to end, and all the parts, just like they are on the record. It was so vivid, it felt real. Then I woke up. It was six-thirty a.m. My brain still in a haze, I realized I'd never heard that song before. My next thought was, *WOW!*

It took me a second to grasp what just happened. I got out of bed, grabbed my bible and went straight to the piano. I played through the song once, to make sure I remembered it. Then looked up the scripture and began writing. The song was completely written before 7 a.m. Such an amazing experience to have received that gift, and then had the privilege of sharing it with the world. Once again, I experienced the tangible love of God.

> *"Music speaks what cannot be expressed. Soothes the mind and gives it rest. Heals the heart and makes it whole, flows from heaven to the soul."*
> —Author Unknown

CONCLUSION

Woven throughout each chapter of this book is the overarching theme of responsibility. The message that you are in control of your destiny. To experience inner *Harmony*, you must first take responsibility for your life. Your thoughts, choices and actions determine your circumstances. They always have and they always will. So, if you want your circumstances to change, you must be the one to change them. Devise a plan by following the instructions in chapter one. Once you've written down your plan, make a commitment to keep your word to yourself, and be consistent as you carry it out.

In the beginning I outlined the importance of rewriting your program. I cannot impress upon you enough, the significance of the subconscious mind because it is the control center of your life. It houses your beliefs and values. It's responsible for storing your long-term memory, your imagination, your intuition, and your fears. The sub-conscious is 95% responsible for your behavior. It influences your thoughts and governs your emotions. It determines whether you succeed or fail in your education. It determines whether you possess the tools to maintain a healthy, loving relationship or not. Your sub-conscious mind is responsible for establishing your belief system, your earning potential, and your physical well-being. It's unfortunate that you did not participate in the act of writing your program. You had no control in the process of establishing your own guidance system. But you are in complete control of the process of changing it.

Achieving a state of inner harmony begins by taking responsibility for your condition. You are the composer and conductor of the symphony that is your life! Even if you were born into poverty and raised in a toxic environment, don't use that as an excuse to remain stuck. Some of the greatest achievers in history came from an underprivileged background. But they didn't let that stop them. They persisted with their passion until they became someone that would change the world.

Oprah Winfrey was born in Mississippi, to a poor, teenage mother. She was molested, and even became homeless at the age of fourteen. The strength and resilience she gained through adversity would shape her into the iconic personality that we all know.

Jim Carrey dropped out of school as a young teen to help support his family, who was living in their van. Both Oprah Winfrey and Jim Carrey are just two examples of what can happen when a person exercises their will instead of being tossed to and fro by the winds of their surroundings.

Remember, repetition is the key to lasting change. Go through each chapter a second time and highlight the parts that resonate with you. Be mindful of using the words *"I am."* They have creative power. Always choose the path of love over fear. Have compassion on those around you and develop the skill of looking at life from their perspective.

Accept yourself for who you are, the good and the not so good. And love that person fully and unconditionally.

Do your best to maintain your *emotional set point* by focusing your mind on the positive and keeping an attitude of gratitude. Practice acceptance by allowing the things you cannot change to be as they are. Don't fight reality. Even in negative situations, there is always a lesson to be learned. Don't allow outside stimuli to govern your emotional state. You make the choice. Choose love. Choose gratitude. Choose Harmony.

ABOUT THE AUTHOR

Jackie Gouché is a mother, mentor, minister, musician, singer, songwriter, and author. She has traveled to six of the seven continents while signing behind some of the most notable names in the music industry. These names include Elton John, Michael Jackson, Tina Turner, Diana Ross, Chaka Kahn, Quincy Jones, Patti LaBelle, Jill Scott, Yolanda Adams, and a host of others.

Jackie has also authored four books, including *How Would I Know*, her autobiography; *True Worshippers*, an in-depth treatise on the biblical aspect of Praise and Worship; *Raising Kings*, Jackie candidly shares her experience as the mother of Daniel (D Smoke) Farris, Sir Darryl Farris (Inglewood Sir), and Davion Farris. These three young, Grammy-nominated artists are taking the music industry by storm. Hopefully, you have enjoyed reading her current book, *Harmony: Cultivating Inner Peace*.

www.ingramcontent.com/pod-product-compliance
Lightning Source LLC
Chambersburg PA
CBHW051230120626
46547CB00013B/1578